The Magic Box:
A Hypnotic Bedtime Story

Written by Amy Arvary, M.ht.

Illustrated by Jason J. Nicholas

Copyright © 2012 Amy Arvary

All rights reserved.

ISBN-10: 0615821642

ISBN-13: 978-0615821641

Dedication

This book was inspired by a very special human, my daughter, Izabella.

Your love set me free and I am grateful for every step of our journey together.

Your light ignited mine.

I love you.

About This Book

What makes this book hypnotic?

This book incorporates all the intricate and necessary parts found in a hypnotic experience. The beginning is designed to relax your child. Once relaxed your child can allow their imagination to create positive scenarios related to their own life. This book includes suggestions for relaxing, feeling confident, problem solving and making healthy decisions.

Why is this book good?

This book was written by a clinical hypnotherapist after witnessing the positive changes that take place in the children she has worked with through the past several years. Regardless of the issue that brought them to her work, each one has experienced an increase confidence and overall more positive attitude. This book is for parents, grandparents, or anyone interested in reading a wonderful story that has the potential of increasing your child's confidence while you teach them a helpful tool- how to relax.

What is helpful to know?

*Something to know is that children wiggle. Unlike adults who relax more still, children may move around. Let them. A suggestion is to just make sure they keep their head on the pillow.

*Also, they may want to see the beautiful illustrations....perhaps they hear the story once with their eyes open and then again with their eyes closed. Let them create their own pictures.

* Emphasize the bold words while reading.

Before we begin, take a moment and get yourself nice and comfortable because I'd like to share a story with you.

It is a **very** special story.

This story is special because it will help you to feel better and to do better. The things that once bothered you will no longer bother you as they may... and you will begin to feel confident enough to do things you once thought too difficult.

So just take a nice deep breath. Breathe in and blow out...

This time take a deep breath in and hold it for 1,2,3 and let it go... good. See how your whole body has already begun to relax?

*Your body is **magnificent**.*

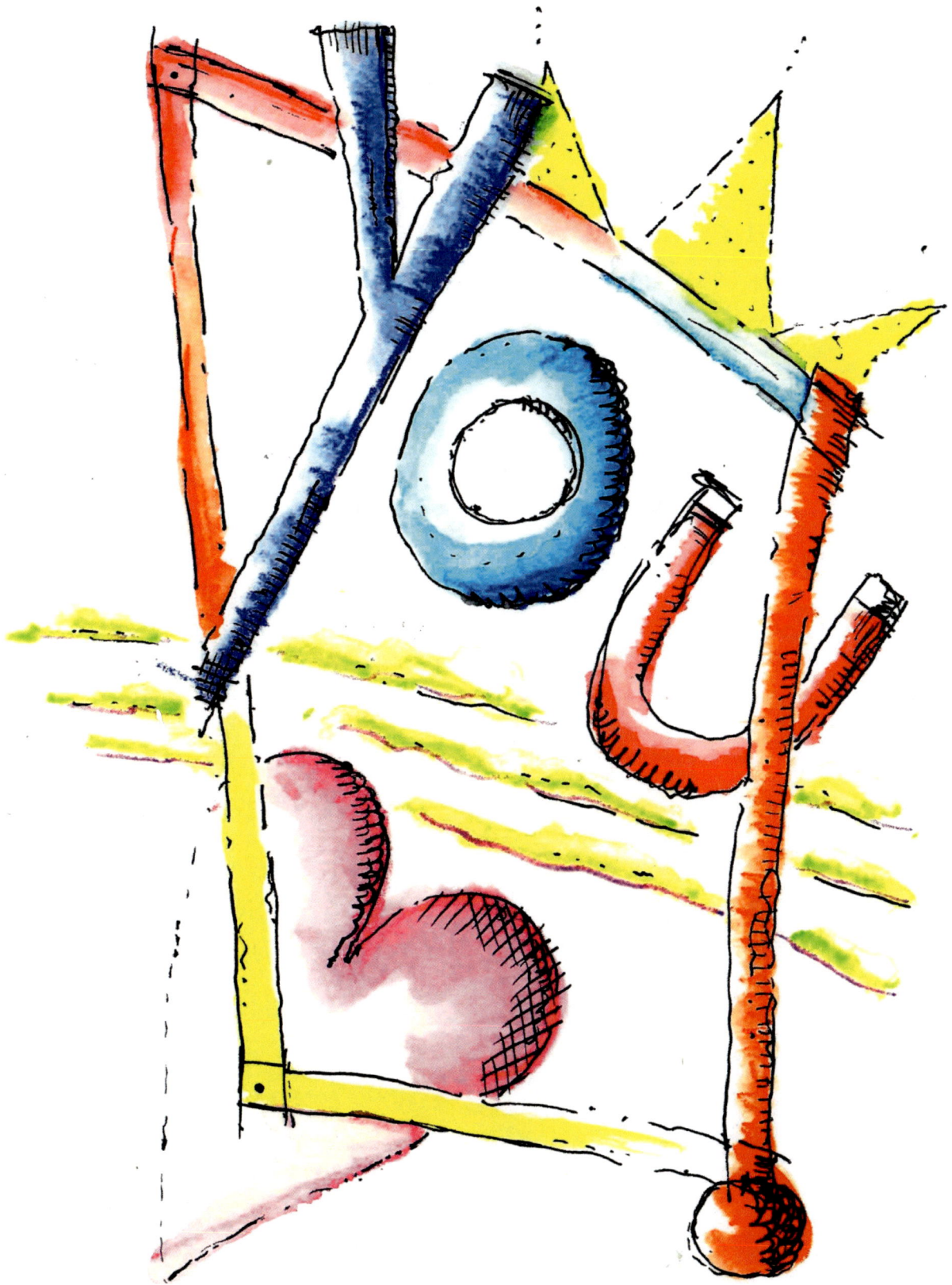

From this moment on, every breath you take will help you get even more comfortable... even more calm. You can feel it as your head gets heavy and drops down a bit... and your neck relaxes- the front and the back of your neck. And that good feeling travels right down over your body... from your head all the way down to your toes... so comfortable and so relaxed.

Now, as your body is so relaxed, imagine standing in a big backyard with lots of green grass and beautiful trees and flowers... maybe there is a pool, maybe there is a swing set or tree house...the sun is shining and it's a beautiful day... just allow your mind to create the picture for you.

Your mind is **magnificent**.

Notice the big stone you are standing on and the stones leading from where you stand to a colorful box sitting under a tree. There are 10 big stones and in a moment you can step on them one at a time ...

*There is something **magical** about the stones.*

When you step on them you will feel yourself get more relaxed and comfortable... even sleepy.

So just enjoy the feeling as you make your way to the box under the tree.

Go ahead now and step on the next stone... the 9th stone...and feel yourself get heavier... try it again now and step on the next stone.

*Y*ou get sleepier and sleepier... step again and get even more relaxed... go ahead and try it again and again ... step on the next stone and feel yourself getting heavier and more relaxed...

Step again and go deeper and deeper...and again...now three stones left... take a step and go deeper... another step...

You are so relaxed as you take the last step now... right up to the colorful box under the tree.

Notice how good you feel right now, under this tree by this magical box and these magical stepping stones... so good... so relaxed and calm. Take a nice deep breath.

Go ahead now and kneel down... kneel down under the tree in front of this magical box. Notice how the colors shine in the sunlight. Notice the colors and the patterns.

Go ahead and put your hands gently on the box. Feel the magic come in through your hands as they begin to tingle and feel warm.

Notice how that feeling travels up your arms and into your shoulders and your head and down to your heart.

Imagine that magic traveling down to your stomach relaxing those muscles and all the way through your body, soothing and relaxing those muscles while you continue feeling calm and happy to be here... enjoying this magic.

Think for a moment about whatever has been bothering you because the answer to your problem is in this box...

Go ahead and open the box.
Look inside the box... it appears empty,
because its magic has given you exactly
what you needed.

Whatever it is that you felt you needed is in you now…whatever frightened you no longer does, whatever worried you no longer does.

The magic in this box filled you with everything you need. You just felt whatever that is and you feel so much better. So much more confident, calmer… so much happier. It is a part of you now.

From this moment on you are aware that the answer to your problems is inside of you. You give yourself permission to feel better... you are more relaxed and ready to make healthy decisions as you move through your life.

*You are **fabulous**!*

So now just rest and dream of all the things you can create and be and do. You are an important part of this world. You just keep getting better and better, so rest now.

When you wake you will feel refreshed and excited to give the world your very best, but for now just relax...

You are fabulous indeed.

Much Love.

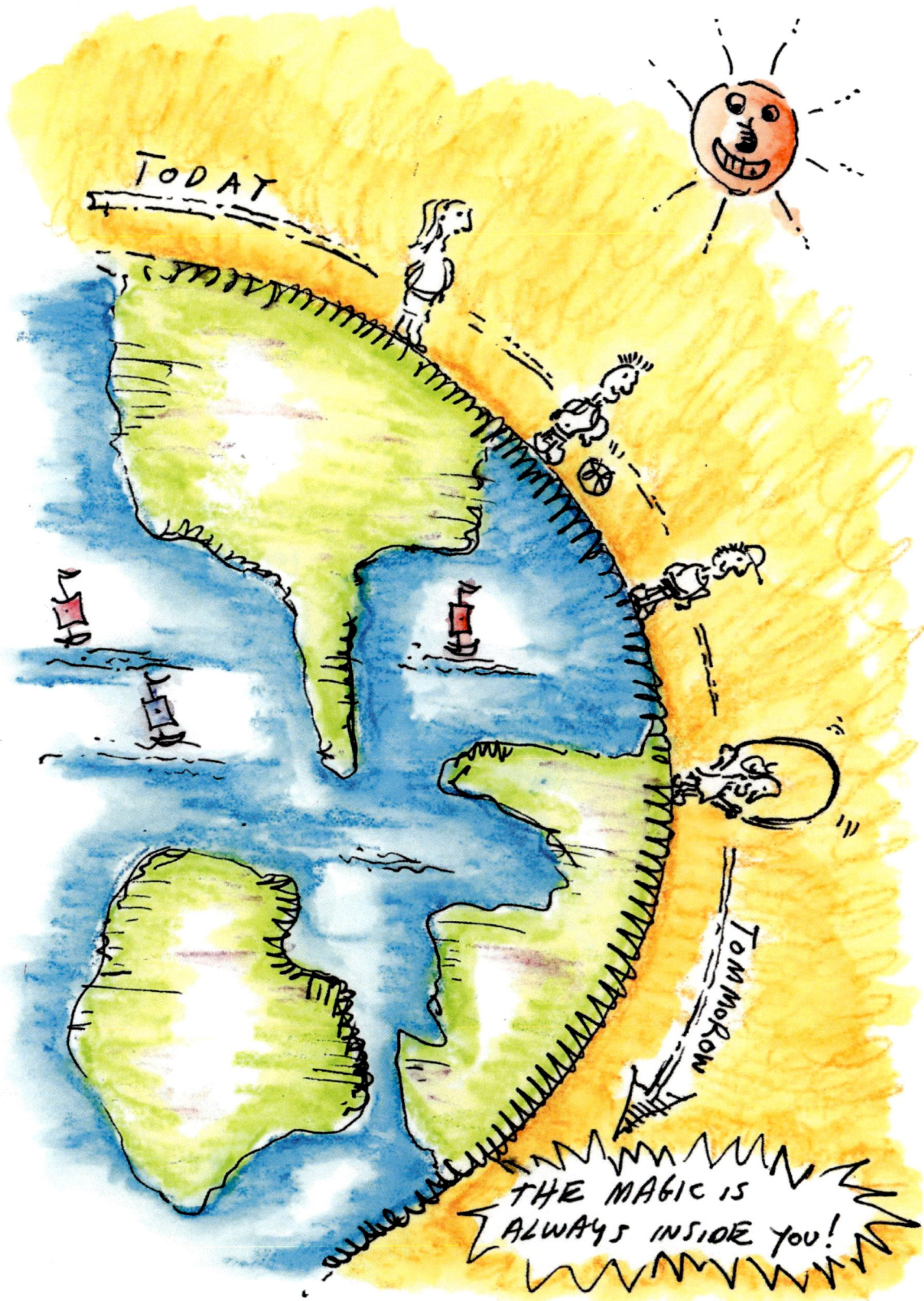

TODAY

TOMMOROW

THE MAGIC IS ALWAYS INSIDE YOU!

25

ABOUT THE ILLUSTRATOR

Born with a pencil in his mouth in 1970, Jason J. Nicholas has always been passionate about exploring his creativity (don't worry, the pencil wasn't sharpened). From his childhood architectural dreams to his heart-warming artwork and humor, he expresses his inner creativity by sharing the gift of his imagination. Some say he is a combination of Mike Brady and Bob Ross with a touch of Dr. Seuss (without the six kids, cool afro, or Wocket in his pocket). Jason is a rugged /outdoorsy husband, super hero cool father, architect, artist, improv actor, and ice cream taste-tester wannabe. Be sure to check out his warmth, wit, and wisdom at www.jasonjnicholas.com or on Facebook at www.facebook.com/JJN.Inklings .

ABOUT THE AUTHOR

Amy Arvary, M.ht. currently lives in New Jersey and spends most of her time growing her daughter and her company Amy Arvary Conscious Style which empowers children, women and men of all ages. As a Master Certified Clinical Hypnotherapist Amy has designed programs that have helped add relief to children and adults world-wide. She is passionate about helping others find their internal strength and calm by learning how to think differently. She enjoys speaking at schools and corporations, teaching how to accelerate improvement and good vibes ;) For more information visit www.AmyArvary.com or call (800)315-5616

Made in the USA
Middletown, DE
11 September 2022